A load of BULL

Dave Bull

A load of BULL

Copyright © 6th March 2013 Dave Bull

All rights reserved.

ISBN-10: 1482572214
ISBN-13: 978-1482572216

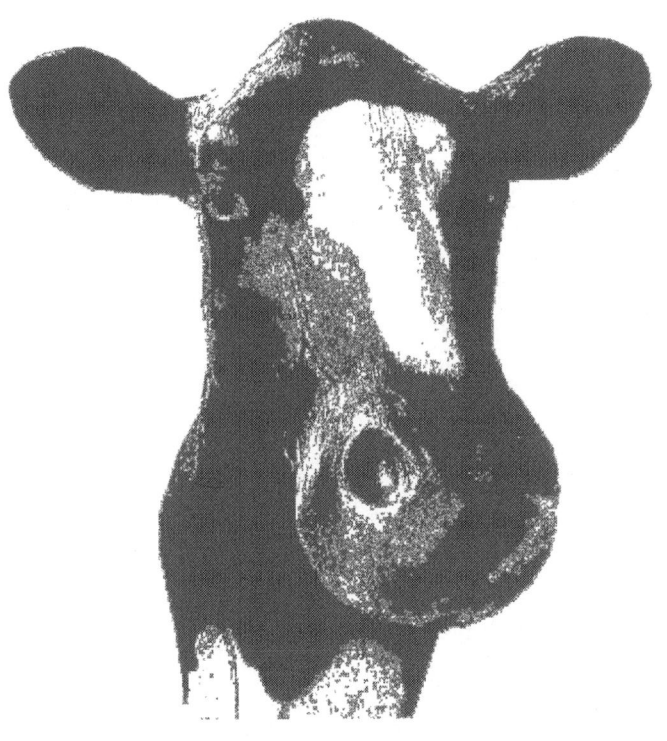

Daisy
A few words of thanks for Daisy the stunt cow without whom this book would not have been possible,
Her professionalism and dedication to her art means that she will live out her life happily guarding a removals depot and I can guarantee that she'll never be eaten…

THANKS

*To Sue Sharpe for her studious appraisal of this book,
and for showing me what commas are for...*

*And...
To everyone who smiles, inside or out...*

FOREWORD

For about half of the time I've lived in Spain, I've known Dave, and enjoyed his off-the-wall writing-style – indeed, have followed with interest his similar life-style. If you're looking for a serious account of life in this very un-European country, then perhaps 'A Load of Bull' is not for you. But who said that life here – or anywhere else, for that matter – was serious?

This book is a collection of anecdotes, many about Spain and the Spanish, some about the experience of being an 'expat,' (not a term I embrace with much joy) and others which could occur in Dorking or Dortmund – but certainly not in Deauville, as the author makes clear his antipathy to our mutual neighbours.

What is common to all Dave's writing is his capacity for enjoyment, undiminished by the setbacks he has encountered along the way, and I don't see how anyone can fail to be amused by his accounts.

Dave has also cultivated a profound love for his adopted Mediterranean stamping ground – I reckon you'll find him dunking croissants into his coffee in Juande's in twenty years' time – and this shines as bright as the Costa Blanca sunshine throughout this unusual narrative.

Malcolm Palmer – author & ornithologist

Dave Bull

Disclaimer

All the characters (apart from me, Daisy and quite a few others) are fictional - unless you recognise yourself - and the author takes no responsibility for anyone lacking the sense of humour to see the funny side of life.
Most of the time I say things with my tongue firmly wedged in my cheek so if I mention shooting a neighbour...it's more than likely a joke, unless I improve my aim anyway...
Enjoy.
Dave Bull

Dave Bull

CONTENTS

Intro. About the author [i]

1. **Life** — Page 1
2. **People** — Page 19
3. **Travel** — Page 28
4. **Women** — Page 33
5. **Spain** — Page 38
6. **Kids** — Page 55

More stuff... Page 58

About the author

Dave Bull has been living and working in Spain since 2000. Now a full-time travel writer he lives with his son, Mitch (and their Labrador, Woopy), on the Costa Blanca penning his experiences and observations on living life as an expat in Spain and on his travels throughout Europe.

Always from his own 'different' perspective, he publishes one of the most successful magazines on the Costa Blanca and has been the Editor of two regional expat newspapers.

His first book *It just is...* was published in 2011 and recounts his life abroad and if you really have nothing better to do, have a read, (and a laugh) about Dave's experiences at the hands of the Spanish - where he reveals, as ever, in his own unique style just what some of us expats get up to in Spain which in Dave's case included getting arrested, getting dumped (often) and having a blind date...with an aunt...

Twitter: @davejbull

FaceBook: Dave Bull

Blog: www.loadofbull.es

Magazine website: www.allabroad.es

Available from www.amazon.co.uk

About **It just is...**

The book follows a year in Dave's life including a good amount of helpful information but delivered in Dave's unique manner that makes it interesting and informative, and of course fun!

Some of what goes wrong for expats in Spain is their own fault...some is not, and Dave tries to distinguish between the two in a self-deprecating manner that makes this book so readable.

It Just Is... aims to help, entertain and amuse expats, those looking to move abroad (not only to Spain) and anyone who just enjoys a good laugh.

'I hope you can see that beneath my dashing good looks, charming exterior and rugged (yet comfy) complexion – is a pig ugly writer waiting to reach lots of interested readers.'

A load of BULL

To Mitch,
Still, and always, my little boy and my friend...
...all 6 feet 7 inches of you!
(Dig, Dig.)
Dad.

Dave Bull

1 LIFE

Someone just asked me the question that if I was on death row what my last meal would be? I said anything that gave me serious diarrhea...

An appeal to all Scots out there wanting independence - think! It´ll affect the rest of us - Union Jack will look crap with no blue in it...

How many kids did/do you know at school that are just dead funny? THAT talent should be encouraged as much as academic ones.

Clocks go back Saturday don't forget-I'm putting mine back 2 hours; figure an extra hour in bed is worth being late for 6 months..

My mum has informed me that I'm in her will so 'not to worry' - I offered to take her shark watching to celebrate but she ain't having it...

It's that time of the day when I reward myself with a cup of tea and a sausage roll... Jimi Hendrix lives on in spirit...

They say it's all in the planning, so...if I'm in a cafe (quite a bit) its ok...cos I'm planning to work... :-)

Well that's another session of dog-dragging over...or jogging with a fat Labrador as it's also known...

So, I'm out running & spot the pretty woman so puff the chest out & up the pace (a lot) & then realise she can see for miles.. So I fake an injury rather than try and keep running...

I just attacked a full English brekky like Spike used to eat a bone in Tom & Jerry #stuffed

Is it just me or does the name for the storm in the States sound like a camp Action Man; 'Superstorm Sandy'...with matching cushions..?

Loving my new tablet...it has given me the freedom to do less, but more often... :-)

Why is there ALWAYS something I desperately need from the Chinese Bazaar shop..?

Judging by the amount of women wearing animal print in this bar I'm guessing that they serve saucers of milk... #Benidorm

If you do nothing else this weekend, make it yours... :)

It was emotional, hurtful & some nasty things were said (by me)...but I've no regrets & I'll try again later to put the quilt cover on...

Like Starbucks etc. I shall be reconsidering my tax commitments...unlike Starbucks I didn't have a choice...

Possibly at the worst Flamenco eve ever...so bad its good, sounds like a cross between the Gypsy Kings & The Wurzels...

The beauty of Twitter is everyone can use it; the danger of Twitter is everyone can use it...

You know it's gonna be a tough day when you start it by punching yourself in the privates getting dressed...Will put the light on next time...

On the subject of health (no idea) can we not cover our 'five a day' by carefully selecting pizza toppings & having a fruit juice with it..?

Mates visiting: we are going for a meal & it's a little different from their normal dining experience... i.e. they won't get a free toy...

Gonna have to go back to Ikea...that's the third shelf I've put up and none of them are straight...

My last school report: "Dave wastes far too much time messing around & too little on the basics..." - I didn't like teaching there anyway...

Ok...one more request to play a game or join a daft app on Facebook and I'm gonna have to name & shame...

Coincidence...? The hamster's disappeared and the dog's not hungry...

Woopy the Labrador has to stop practising her sprint starts while I'm out, all the rugs are piled up at the end of the hall again.

At post office behind Brit woman moaning (in English) at Paco (doesn't speak English) - never a sniper around when you want one is there..?

Confirming earlier comment: I am at THE worst flamenco in Spain...& I now know what it sounds like just outside the gates at Guantanamo...

We just won the pub quiz! I'd like to thank my teammate Kevin, and our silent partner Google...

My ex really knew how to hurt me...she used to come home and show me the receipt...

My book is available on a kindle..! And yes, I'm walking around like Foghorn Leghorn... I say, I say

You gotta love FIFA...I bet when the Titanic went down they said: "it'll be fine...just give it another hour & it'll float...again..."

Just had a lesson in life that I thought I'd pass on so others may learn too: don't bring a chicken chow mein home on a motorbike...

Never in the field of human conflict have I been so bugged by so few. My house is now at war with flies-I asked politely now it's personal...

Lance Armstrong continually denies what everyone knows...is this the modern day version of The Emperors Clothes..?

I tried sailing today & got a bit tangled in the ropes; the instructor looked at me like you would a new born foal trying to walk...

EU have won the Nobel peace prize & José Barroso said it had 'been awarded to all 500 million EU citizens' - that's going on my CV then!

Listening to Stray Cats & using dog's tail as double bass, cat sounds like a symbol when I poke it and the hamster is starting to sweat...

Someone's just reminded me; life's one big lesson....and I've just remembered; I've been bunking off...

Just as I reach 120kph...a wasps strolls across the inside of my helmet visor. Apologies to the highway dept. for the black line...

Wahay! Just broke the lap record at 'Silverstone'! (Or the Gran Alacant coast rd. as it's also known...)

After a few Riojas I must stop shouting "nun-night!" to all the birds nesting, I think the rabbits may be jealous...

You know those fairies that come along in the night & clear up..? I seem to have the anti-fairy visiting, nightly...

I´ve had all my hair cut short... how come all the hair on the salon floor is brown while the stuff left on my head is grey..?

She wanted me, I felt the same way. It was instant & we went straight back to my place... & that's how we ended up with Woopy the Labrador...

Just did a great gig Elvis, Oasis songs & more - I did sound good but great venue & superb acoustics -I might have another shower in a bit...

Putting up low shelf & a bent drill doesn´t help. My wall now looks like I've shot 3 of the 7 dwarves...

Advice for men: if a woman asks how she looks in before/after shots at beauty parlour DO NOT answer "the same" trust me, it hurts...

Some things in life should shouted from the roof tops & others that are better to shut up & be smug about, I'm being smug...for now

The last (only) thing I remember the PT telling me was, "drink plenty of fluids"...I haven't let him down on that one... #Rioja

Signing copy of my book a lady said "you never know 1 day it could be worth something" I told her to think positive & hope I get run over...

Is anyone willing to help me campaign to reinstate the primary school rule of "you kissed me so you gotta marry me..." but for adults..?

I'm in the bank being stared out by a 3 year old in a pushchair...bet he's called Damian...

At the library for a book - choice of two: Quantum physics for the 21st century or Understanding Women... so, science section it is then...

Life's full of mysteries...just educated my son showing that a cake goes hard & a biscuit soft...so where does that leave Jaffa Cakes..?

As is traditional on my birthday we shall be playing kiss-chase tonight - all welcome but sorry fellas the male quota (of 1) is full... ;)

Learnt tonight to drink is athletic, I used to be a sprinter & later middle distance...I'm now the bloke on the long jump...with the flag...

All birthday kisses (gratefully, & willingly accepted) will be passed on to my beautiful partner...just as soon as I meet her... :)

Kiss-chase: Thanks for the great response, all 3 of you...my mum, an odd lady (with a limp) & the guy who thought it was a tribute band...

Had a great birthday & as is traditional at this point in the evening may I say, I BLOODY LOVE YOU!

Know your limits: juggling oranges is one thing, knives is another... 6 stitches & advice from the doc which included growing up...

Some things are just so wrong...I mean if wine was meant to come in cartons surely we'd get it from red & white cows..?

Just smacked my head on another low doorway...it can´t be my fault that the rest of the world is short...

Have you noticed that evolution has gone full circle & we´re now walking like Egyptians...but with a smartphone in each hand...

Congratulations Peugeot for making what must be the securest motorcycle storage space in the world... b@#$%&/s!

*After going A*** over T** again during the night I've come to the decision, I either need a new rug...or a different colour dog...*

If dogs could whistle... My dog is shuffling sideways with furtive glances as I eat a Yorkie (bar not Terrier)

Something tells me that my brekky diet of a coffee a fag a mars bar & another fag needs tweaking... (Btw for yanks out there fag=cigarette)

When the organiser of expo asked me if I wanted to go to her spit-roast today I wasn't sure what to expect...

The line in my book 'stayed in on my own with a DVD and a box of tissues...' needs changing - it was a sad film...okay?

Being single dad I sometimes have to play the 'mum' role, so I've sent my son with wheelbarrow to buy choc while I watch CSI. Close ladies?

Right, tonight (indoors) I'm wearing a sarong...don't ask, very liberating but every time I try and step over something I fall over...

Nature always wins... Riding through countryside on motorbike & just met a beetle coming the other way - head on. & it wasn't Ringo...

Benefits of living in Spain: coffee prevents frostbite - I've been drinking Spanish coffee for years & never once had it...

Here's an idea: how about we remake Cool Hand Luke...? I'll volunteer for the role - so long as we can use Cadburys Crème Eggs this time..?

It's taken him a while but my son has finally realised that no...We haven't got a dishwasher...

Lessons for teenagers #14356487 - when the bin is overflowing that is exactly the right time to stop putting more stuff in it...

Healthy diet under way...drinking juice only tonight- grape juice...actually crushed grape juice, ok...wine...but it's a start...?

I'm all for standing up for my rights & living in a democracy but if the authorities tell me I CAN'T work today, I can go with that...

Dunno what the washing machine's problem is...why can't it just do its job & return my clothes the same size & colour as when they went in..?

I'll always remember my first wedding, if only for the fact that the cake lasted longer than we did...

Some of you may have realised by now the phrase 'hammer it home' - when talking about me - has nothing to do with sex...

I just looked at the veggie menu & I mean come on, if we weren't meant to eat animals they wouldn't have made them out of meat would they..?

I don't normally complain but I just had a steak so rare that it mooed...and I think it ate my chips...

Woohoo! After peaking yesterday it's now wind-down time as we head for the weekend!

Serious training & I've discovered on the net that even Linford Christie liked the odd fry-up...I'll be moving his routine on a portion

The problem with being tall when it rains is brollies are the exact same height as my eyes; fortunately I already have a Labrador...

If SabadellCAM can't get their act together I'll be sorely tempted to take my debts elsewhere...

It's not easy being a genius...Cleaning and I just locked myself out of the house with the keys (& dog) inside... Cafe till my lad wakes - at about 1...

I've tried my very best to fix the oven but I guess it needs something a bit more technical than me shouting, "COOK YOU B@#%&*D!"

My life is a set to achieve as much as poss. before life's egg timer runs out, trouble is I don't know how much sand is in it...

Just sat the Labrador down for her 2012 appraisal...I will be mentioning in her 2013 one that she fell asleep during this one...

A peaceful sunny afternoon & neighbour opposite has got his strimmer out. In response I'm getting the replica bow & arrow off the wall...

Gotta do some DIY later which usually, and unintentionally, turns into a Frank Spencer Tribute act...

Just opened a 15 year old bottle of Rioja and I'm not saying it's good but I wouldn't mind if tomorrow is groundhog day...

Just been out training and disaster...I've pulled a muscle in my shoulder and now I can't reach the Marmite...

Following my small business tweet I've had a mix of responses including one urging a revolution...told him I can't, I haven't got a beret...

It is with great sadness that I have to announce that following a long battle I must admit defeat. And sleep without a quilt cover again...

Aaaagh...! I'm no techy, but I'm making an educated guess that a Muller Corner (inc jam) is not good for a laptop keyboard...

Due to a late night I've decided to introduce a pause between each press up in today's training session....of about 6 hours...

Some days you just have to accept responsibility & knuckle down...fortunately, as far as I'm concerned, today is not one of them...

Support small business: unselfishly tonight I'll visit many bars as poss. & an Indian restaurant a cab firm & tomorrow the Pharmacia

So much to do yet so little time, although... so much beach & even less time... Beach it is then, glad that's sorted

That was close...I thought I spotted a cloud but it's just another neighbour having a barbecue...

There's better ways to wake up from sun bathing....just been French-kissed by a Labrador...

After being financially abused I've realised that it's cheaper to drink jet fuel than buy a coke in McDonalds...

Planning... I've had two ceiling fans fitted in the lounge today but when I put both on its like sitting beneath an incoming Chinook...

Loads of work to do so I'm using the 'it might not be sunny tomorrow so I'd better go the beach today' plan- which I'll use again tomorrow...

Worked all (most) of the day & I'm slumped over desk when I reach out & discover bottle wine. It's a sign & one I'd be a fool to ignore...

I know...I know... it's time I grew up and I will, tomorrow...straight after my Sugar Puffs...

You ever have one of those days when you can't get a song out of your head? I'm having one... & unfortunately it's the theme from Rainbow...

So here I find myself again...another roof terrace bar in the sun, drinking mojitos & chatting...don't you just hate routine..?

Just dropped another plate...but why the bloody hell did I instinctively stick my foot out to stop it? @#%&! It's smarting a bit...

After a long, tense and sometimes noisy battle littered with expletives....I've got the quilt cover on!

Life's not simple: had a clear out of all my old clothes: sorted, folded, and bagged & in the recycle bin...but I haven't see my watch since...

Growing flowers (not)... I wouldn't mind but they live quite happily on the Chinese shops terrace until I buy them - then its hari kari...

Terrific...after mentioning flowers this morning my Labrador has decided to put the new ones out of their misery...by eating them...

Why on earth is everything going so slow today?! PC, Car, Time, Work, Kettle...oh...wait a minute, it's me...

Imagine life begins on a bus & we're told that it'll stop once. When we get back on we die we'd make the most of it wouldn't we?

Just settled on the beach alone & realised what that niggle thing was I'd had in the back of my mind - I was supposed to pick everyone up...

I could be wrong...but I think I'm looking at my bottle of 2004 Rioja with just a little too much affection...

I'm just giving some new plants their last rites...i.e. I'm planting 'em... I give them a week before they prefer death to living here...

Just back from gym & used new machine for 30min that left me feeling sick—but it's great & does everything, mars bars, kit kats, coke...

Fighting the urge to go to beach, but I'm sure someone somewhere said that now & again it's best to lose a battle to advance-I surrender...

Just off for an interview on Viva TV....I do hope the green room is prepped for me....Jelly Tots aren't that hard to find...

You know you're having one of those days when... I just dunked my cigarette in my tea while the biscuit is waiting nicely by the ashtray...

You know you're middle-aged when...you've just bought slippers for the first time after years of fighting it...bugger.

Just whipped a fly with a wet towel...broke coffee mug and a vase - can report that fly is doing well and continuing with its day...git.

Just spent 20 minutes looking for a sweatshirt that I was sure I hadn't thrown out...to discover I was wearing it...

I helped a lady in the Chinese shop & put a dog bed back on the top rack for her...pushing a kennel off the other side & on to other lady...

Chilling on the terrace before work...be handy if the gardener could get a quieter leaf-blower...or am I being too picky..?

Woohoo!! Explain later...but still Woohoo!!

SATURDAY BREAKFAST SHOW Do I go smart casual...or turn up in 'Tigger' themed pyjamas..?

I May not be a sommelier but I have been taste testing tonight and discovered that a good Rioja goes very well with...pork scratching's...

The law of nature says I have to grow old...but there's nothing saying I have to grow up... :-)

It's funny how helping someone can turn a pretty crap day into a good one :)

I've had a great day writing my second book, and it's stirred up some memories although the ex-rent boy's proposition still keeps me awake...

Is it just me...or does everyone suddenly stop what they're doing and think, 'f***! ...I'm 45', or similar..?

As I stood by the window & stretched (like a gymnast dismounting a pommel horse) naked this morning - I wished I'd drawn the curtains...

After a day of cleaning, ironing, washing & cooking I have a sudden urge for chocolate, a hot bath & to paint my toes while watching a DVD...

So that's me & the clean quilt had another fight....it looks like it's got a hippo hiding in it...but I'll beat it into shape while I sleep...

Feeling lucky today....woke up this morning with no feeling from the waist down...turned out it was my Labrador asleep on my legs...

If something is worrying or getting you down...find something funny in it - works for me! :-)

Just taking the motorbike to Alicante...in a box. I don't know if I need a mechanic or a magician...

I've just made a marmite and onion sandwich by mistake...I wouldn't recommend it...

Been a long day but now I've walked the dinner, prepared the dogs for work and put my laptop in the oven... Ready for another day!

Going to get my next super hi-tech phone in a bit...but with all this technology can't they make one with a prescription touch screen...?

4 weeks & no cigarettes but Jaffa Cakes coming in now by the truck load!

2 PEOPLE

Just stepped in front of a very slow moving car that tooted for way too long, so I shouted back in French - to deflect blame on my homeland ;)

I've just had a curse put on me by a gypsy woman...explain later, unless I get turned into a frog - in which case any princesses on twitter?

Have you got one of those annoying mates like I have? Has to go one better? If I've been to Tenerife he's been to Elevenarife...

Take a moment to think of the plight of tall people will you..? I got up this morning & stretched - forgetting the ceiling fan was on...

My last girlfriend was so disappointed after she invited me to a 'BDSM session' - how was I to know it wasn't a driving school..?

To all the Arsenal fans out there...we're laughing with you, honestly... ;-)

I have a confession...I've got a French mate...

The real new generation Europeans are the kids of us expats, bilingual, bicultural and open minded. We've started something amazing... #expat

People-watching now & the early conclusion is that you can tell an awful lot about someone by which way round they wear their baseball cap...

Yes I'm wearing a polar grade fleece on a sunny day in Spain, yes I bought it from a convincing Moroccan - he's bringing me a sledge later..

I've just had an idea how politicians could drastically cut the carbon footprint in every country. Why don't they just shut up?!

She'd just flown in & was short with very long legs, a slim neck and a big nose...my type of bird, but then I've always liked flamingos...

At Alicante port...People have got to stop overdoing the Botox...I nearly chucked one woman back in the water...

Today's entertainment has moved the crowd -to another bar, not saying she's bad but imagine Edith Piaf singing My Way while being stabbed...

Off for what should be an interesting interview: the last time I stood in front of this guy - It was as the defendant...

There's nothing like waking up on a Saturday morning with her looking at me like she adores me... Time for her walk I guess...

How fortunate I am to have a Labrador that sleeps like a walrus, in a coma, with a heavy cold...

Never leave a Spanish butcher alone with your Sunday joint...if you do, when you get it back it'll fit in the cd rack nicely...

In a rush this morning so a Spanish friend offered to park my car for me....but that's a bit like Gary Glitter offering to babysit...

Going to rugby practice for 1st time in years tomorrow - can I just say how much I respect you big, strong, fast, guys...

Being typically British...I have a sudden interest in cycling, & an unlikely new hero called "Wiggins" - the French ain't gonna like it :-)

Just read Lee Child, One shot, again...good old Jack, women wanna love him & men wanna be him.

She's pushed me too far this time...after catching her in bed (not alone) I've kicked her out. No more Bonios or long walks either...

Been stuck behind a cyclist for 2km can I remind them - wearing Lycra & shaving your legs does not necessarily make you faster...or narrower

That´s the third time my motorbike´s been knocked over by an idiot parking...I caught them this time. It was the Guardia...so I said ´thanks´...

Tonight I have the wine, the finger food, the music & the sunset to enjoy with two females. But I've still got to FrontLine them first...

You have to question evolution when my dog can do THAT to herself (in front of everyone) and sound like she´s enjoying it so much...

You gotta luv em...the looky looky man today gave me his best spiel as to why I should buy a family size pack of socks, while on the beach..

Love it! Just passed the back of a Chinese restaurant & saw two guys playing draughts...using diff colour tea-light candles as pieces

Later I'll be joined by Ruby Murray-all the way from Delhi -along with boiled rice & naan...so long as Suni's scooter makes it up the hill...

Great...the golf pro has just told me what's wrong: I'm standing too close to the ball...after I've hit it...

After what's just happened I am willing to bet that even Her Maj (the queen) swears her head off when she stubs her toe on the bed..?

We didn't expect to find a nude sunbather in the dunes this early...I don't imagine he was expecting a wet Labrador would land on him either.

Are England players getting younger..? I'm sure Oxlade-Chamberlain had to hold hands with that kid as they walked out in case he got lost...

I've ended up just how my old form tutor said I would if I didn't listen to him... It's just a shame it took so long...

I'm not saying my mate is a wimp but a jelly fish just stung him and he came running out of the sea...on top of the water, screaming...

Chilling looking at mountains, beach & listening to waves. Next door is Karaoke -like getting a date with Cameron Diaz & she's got headache...

If beach guys insist on standing on top a dune with shorts round ankles (like a proud Meer cat holding a walnut) I insist on laughing...

I still love her... My mum was asked by a local newspaper in UK to list her fave 3 books of all time. She forgot include mine.... #bless...

According to a recent survey (mine...just now) men are in their prime at the age of 45...

Ok first day with the personal trainer...I wonder if I take her some flowers and a bacon sandwich she'll go easy on me..?

Mates from UK asked if they should remove shoes in house-I said this is Spain u need to chill out & remove your shoes outside of house...

Being a dad means always being there...i.e. ready with you credit card when the phone rings...

So far today I've had a Russian girl called Ker plunk (I think) email she loves me & a US soldier in Afghan who has 24$ mill to share #lucky

Expat men. We come to Spain. Revive our old footy or rugby skills by joining vets team. Visit nice new A & E dept. Retire...again #Spain

The er...working girl at the roundabout has just made me an offer I couldn't decipher...or probably afford... #Spain

Pepe insists, a car is a car - When I said he'd be better off buying a van to put his sheep in, he said, 'no, I always wanted this Mercedes...'

If ducks were hens: had a reader ask today if I could complain (in Spanish) to the Spanish post office...because they don't speak English...

Bloke has just sworn at everyone & staggered out the door & thrown up. His mate said, 'its ok...he's on holiday' - that's fine then...!

A neighbour returned to UK after ten years here, his reason: 'I love Spain but the way they do things is so Spanish'...

Irony: 'there's too many immigrants (in UK) taking & giving nothing back...' said Steve (the cash in hand expat builder) to me just now...

As a mark of respect to my old Cub Scout leader Tamar....tomorrow I shall polish my woggle...

Pulled over & cop shouts 'get out of car with hands visible' I get out put hands on roof & 2 cop mates fall out cop car laughing

Please understand that the line in my book, 'she was holding my meat and couldn't stop laughing', is about a butcher's assistant...ok?

They say there's a book in all of us...my dog has seven, she ate another blockbuster last night...

Printer said he'd deliver my magazines Monday. I sent him a text first thing Monday to ask what time he'd get here. He said: Wednesday

Asking me not to worry about money is a bit like going to weight-watchers and saying 'don't bother, loads of blokes love fat birds...'

Spanish logic wins... Said to the guy who'd hit my car 3 times parking his 'could have got a bus in there' he said 'why park a bus here?'

Just spent the morning with a sommelier & had a glass or two of champers...1988 Krug, 600€\bottle he's gonna be gutted when it's my round...

...and I'm sure the sommelier won't mind when he comes to our house that we don't need a corkscrew to open wine...we use scissors...

We are lucky the Spanish don't get road rage....it'd be like the Wild West around here...

I'm in a bar and what must be Lovejoy's Spanish brother has just walked in...

Oh. An (elderly) gay man who used to run the chippy has just informed me he'd like to have 'battered my sausage' -take it as a compliment..?

A beautician said today that I need to drink more fluids to help look after my skin...does she think I drink lager for fun..?!

I reckon the woman in the bar who has 'inssshisted' she sings 'I will survive' on karaoke after getting up from floor...is having good hols

Amazing... there's a bloke in the bar who can't speak Spanish but fortunately 'has got all the words'-I've got a guitar but I can't play it...

Spent a good time today with Spain's top wine expert...todays tip? Any cheap wine will taste good with cheese... I love my job

The bloke in my local CAM bank is that bleeding miserable I'm sure he's had a charisma by-pass...

'Despite my protests I was heading for the cooler' (the only way I can get my name in the same sentence as Steve McQueen)

Maybe a mistake to say that my book would be more valuable if I got run over...so far dodged 3 cars & a mobility scooter my mum was driving

3 TRAVEL

I feel like Bear Grylls, practicing survival skills for the dangers of wilderness when we do the bike ride -ok...I'm sewing button on a shirt...

I don't know what the fuss is about 1500km bike ride we're doing, I mean, its France to Gibraltar so it's all downhill, or am I missing summat.?

I've decided...I need a hat - all the great explorers had one; Dr Livingstone, Indiana Jones, Sid James...

On the bus to Madrid & I think making egg sandwiches for the journey may have been a bad idea...

Decision time at Tarragona bus station - I'll get on the first bus I come to...please not France!

I was going to go and discover Zaragoza this week...but I gather someone's already done it....

So far so good just a (huge) dead dog in the rd. to deal with and an amoeba driving a white van...

Ok, we're off. If I'm not in Valencia by 9pm head down N332 to look for me, oh and bring a shovel...

An afternoon in Alicante sampling the cafe and culture...I don't charge for all this research either...

A weekend in Benidorm is an experience like no other in Spain; you´ve heard of the town that never sleeps...welcome... to the one that likes a lie in

Benidorm is unlike any other Spanish city...unique in a sandals & vest with a pint kinda way...

After a wild night on the Tizer at the start of the fiestas, I'm up and out & ready to go...unfortunately Benidorm isn't...yet. #Benidorm

On the Tram via & what is it about Metros that everyone avoids eye contact...except the bloke opposite who's been on the happy cake..? #Spain

Right, Benidorm here I come... Got a short story to write...could be very short... in fact, you just read it... ;)

Tomorrow they're sending me to Granada for the weekend...and I don't think it's the TV studios either...

The Lie-In, The Witch and the New Wardrobe Or... A weekend Discovering Granada

I'm not saying it's cold in Granada this morning but I just passed a penguin...either that or you've got short nuns around here...

My first time in Andalucía and I must say... You've kept the garden nice

Driving through the pine forests of the Sierra Nevada, & listening to George Harrison...it don't get better

The coach driver just made a 'short diversion to collect a passenger' - 30 mins to get his son from school...

One common mistake travellers make is loading too much weight in the backpack; I'm resolving the problem now on the coach, by eating it...

Gotta be said, the guy at ticket office in bus station was very helpful & nice...promised me a seat on my own up front- think I'm driving...

On bus sat next to possibly Giant Haystack & Hattie Jacques' love child, there was not a lot of room at all...

My last trip involved a wrestler, an operating room, high heels, a lot of shampoo & (possibly) Joey Barton´s mum... Me in Murcia coming soon

Travelling & the idea of 2 days in West Midlands didn´t appeal until the editor slapped me (twice) & pointed at map of Spain, oh THAT Murcia...

Just been on a march against the cuts in Murcia...didn't mean to, I crossed the road to buy a banana milkshake & got caught up in the flow...

I'm not saying Murcia is strange or anything but I've just overtaken a guy who was on a bike...and I'm walking...

Tourist Info Benidorm´s said the biggest problem for Brits abroad last year: they forgot which hotel is theirs...

You'd think after I've made the effort to come to a nature park that the birds & stuff could at least show up...Less WWF & more WTF! #Spain

Just broke the photographers' rule no.1 at venue & run out of space on memory card...as a photographer I make a darn good writer...

The introduction of a hammock to an otherwise tranquil evening has turned a Spanish nirvana into a Rioja-soaked foul-mouthed battleground...

Just been in traffic jam stuck behind a woman continually using poorly-aimed screen wash jets....I was on my motorbike... #refreshed

A load of BULL

Missed the point... expat mate just got back from visiting Spain's oldest & biggest winery & excitedly described it as 'a huge Threshers'...

Yes! Yes! Yes! I'm going to Paris next week - expenses paid! Yabbadabba-f****** -do! But I'm cool about it...

If you use the phrase 'gay Paris' as it was originally intended it still applies... One place you must tick off...before you clock off...

Not only is Paris home to the arts but it should be remembered that it also gave us heroes such as Clouseau and Pepe le pew...

Don't you love foreign languages? Tonight I'm in an expat bar listening but not understanding Geordie...

My first night out in a Brit Bar in Spain for years... I'm just too southern. I need to get used to being called 'love' 'flower' & 'duck'...

4 WOMEN

Listen, if there's one thing I know about women it's...nope, sorry gone again...

So that's 26€ for conditioner! How on earth can women afford to live...?! I could have bought something shiny, like a gadget, with that...

As my knowledge of a woman increases - it's directly proportional to my understanding of her decreasing...

I'm not doing any more blind dates...ever. Last night it was Zenka, from somewhere with a funny alphabet- who needed a shave more than me...

There is nothing better than a beautiful woman waking you up with your first coffee...trouble is she then goes and serves someone else...

A date; I didn't want to look desperate for sex. I got ready & checked the mirror & looked like a bloke desperate for sex...

Languages: There I was talking about oral sex with a Señora I didn´t know...later found out she was talking about playing a mouth organ...

All the talk of 50 shades of grey is about sex, and all I hear is BDSM...so where does the driving school fit in...?

Languages are tricky...say to an English woman "I'd love to meat you" and you could end up with a slap...or a slapper..?

Watching the footy AND tweeting, you see ladies? Some of us men can multi tisk...sod it...

NEVER slow down a Spanish mum on the school run, she'll tailgate you & melt the back of your head with her eyes while waving her arms...

I discovered, by accident, how much my ex-girlfriend loved me when she came home & found me fixing motorbike in lounge...note 'ex'...

Just been with the PT...She didn't agree with my argument that if god had wanted us to run everywhere, he wouldn't have invented buses...

Spain has something special for me I'm sure...she's just hiding well...

Apparently there's someone out there for everyone....YOU CAN COME OUT NOW?!

At perfume dept. of El Corte Ingles & respect to women working here -how do they stop their heads from tipping forward with all that make up?

Saturday...I'm sitting watching F1 eating a curry, stroking the dog with my foot...& women say we can't do more than one thing at a time...?

Spanish women are all so unbelievably gorgeous, classy & Cosmo...if they'd just step down to my level... #Spain

Unfortunately, according to MY stars...the most opportune time for me to meet the woman of my dreams is...happy hour...

Discovered over the weekend, there are two theories as to how to argue with women...also found out that neither works...

Although the females in my life show me undying love, like a cuddle and pant a lot...they have 2 too many legs...

just been chatted up...the fact that she was here with SAGA and couldn't remember her name let alone mine did spoil the moment a little...

Following another dispute between Venus & Mars my next book will be along the lines of a Moody Blues song...'Nights while I sat in...'

Is it a bad thing that when I see a beautiful woman, a mini Leslie Phillips sits on my shoulder and says 'ding dong?'...?

The waitress here is called Anna - thanks to her badge, and is gorgeous - thanks to her mum and dad...

Maybe my fault... after she cooked a wonderful meal & put me in front of a movie with wine I should have stayed conscious for the finale...

I know we men can never experience the pain of child birth...but you ladies will never know how it feels to catch your willy in your zip....

This year I've had more beautiful women in my bedroom than ever. Although some (ok, all) were accompanied by an estate agent...

Another first last night....had an intense discussion with a beautiful woman about what clothes you can and can't put on a cold wash...

Is it just a bloke thing that our eyes go on scan mode (shelf by shelf) when we open the fridge...or do girls do that too...?

5 SPAIN

Sitting outside on a terrace, in a t-shirt, drinking coffee & watching the sunrise has got to be the way so start the day...so I am...

Guess whose son passed his driving test today!? ...and guess whose dad has hidden the car keys..?

Gotta hand it to my mate Mark Heyes who, following an argument with a car door will now only be able to count to 9.75 using his fingers...

That bloody moment...when after walking smugly around town- you arrive at your destination & someone says "your flies are undone..."

I may have been over zealous with the clothes clear out & with everything else in the wash I'm left with a choice of a wet suit or a towel...

As he walked through the cafe doorway, smiling at the pretty woman inside, Dave wished for just one thing: that he'd opened the door first...

I am in a cafe with what I can only guess is the Spanish Women's institute & can now appreciate how Michael Caine felt in The Ipcress File...

Just got pinned against a wall by a woman who stepped backwards & had a folded (& sharp) umbrella under her arm - possibly Zorro's mum....

The good news is I've got my new Kindle...but I've just discovered one way it's not as good as a book - killing flies...

Romanians, I'm all for free enterprise but I don't see a demand for tissues to be available at traffic lights...now Crème Eggs I could...

Spain: Did you know? The name Spain evolved from the word Ispania, which means the land of rabbits

All I want to do is read, I don't care if it's written on the back of a toilet door...if it's worth writing, it's worth reading

You gotta love a country where the shop assistant will make you wait while she snogs her boyfriend who came in after you...

Two tips that are essential to enjoy your expat experience: 1. do what they do & 2. Do it when they do it...

Dear god, I'm at a Brit Bar watching Eggheads....if you are going to strike me down, get on with it...

During the boom many adapted the kids phrase, 'when I grow up...' to 'when I move to Spain I'm gonna be a builder/mechanic/plumber' & did

Lost in translation at hairdressers, I said 'Yes' when I thought she said 'pocito?" She had actually said "corto?' It'll grow...

Biggest mistake expats in Spain make when starting a business is to follow the 'Field of Dreams' theory - build it & they'll come...

I just had lunch with a Spanish family & now fully understand & appreciate why they need a siesta... #stuffed

Either Sabadell has a terrific sense of irony after CAM takeover...perhaps the logo says it all..? "Bs"...

Get to know Spain and you get to love Spain

The summer may be gone but the beach is still here...

COSTA-POLITAN in Spain there are no 'foreigners' the people you will encounter in Spain will be interesting....

Welcome to Spain, just 41 sunbathing days till Xmas :)

If you've never had a breakfast in a busy Spanish cafe...remember school dinners in the dining hall...& double the volume...

2 minutes ago I was sat on a terrace full of Spanish. In the last 120 seconds we have experienced exactly 9 drops of rain...& now I'm alone

We've decided, in my house, that if the sun can make an effort to shine tomorrow...we'll make an effort to treat it like a Sunday

Expats are curious folk...its spitting rain & one just said he came here to get away from "that!" - 2nd time we've had rain...since February

*I met Miss Spain today...can I confirm the judges got it bang on... *Sid James growl...*

Reason #6,452,481 for living in Spain: Off to work, which means I´ve got to ride my motorbike around the Spanish...

I'm starting a cult...We'll worship the sun & the sea in a place where food & family come first - join now & become an expat

Being an expat watcher is like being an ornithologist & I've just spotted the white socked sandal walker (AKA: 'dad' or 'uncle')

After a hot dry summer we have cleansing fresh rain, the Spanish govt may have its faults but their weather policy is spot on...

During the boom it wasn't only the property developers rubbing their hands at the sight of Brits arriving. So were the breweries...

The Spanish people can be complicated...why do they eat crabs with their hands but croissants with knife & fork..?

Moving to Spain? One thing that you may not have considered is you might soon wish that cicadas had a volume switch...

Some banks never learn...I'm in the queue in CAM Bank for the one cashier available - watching the other one outside...having a fag...

Spain, a country where it's considered dangerous to change lanes on a roundabout but ok to buy a chainsaw in Aldi...

Spanish history: I don't know about you but I couldn't've lived in Spain B.C. Must have been horrendous... (That's Before Coffee btw)

Can I assure Carl Fogarty that he still holds the lap record at Alicante Airport for getting a Ford Focus from the car park to Arrivals...

Spanish banks are skint but still tell clients to return other day & time to pay bills (put money in the bank!)...is one of us a bit thick..?

I'd like to take this moment to inform speech therapists that the rain in Spain does not fall mainly on the sodding plain

They've finally painted the old flour factory in Alicante...either that or there's been a huge explosion...

I've just been scrumping...Spanish style - loadsa stuff! Hardly carry it all on bike, although I think the sheep was going a little far...

Just spent ten minutes trying to work out what ATOV stood for on a banner, then realised I'm looking at it from the back...it's early ok.. (VOTA = Vote in Spanish)

There's just something so expat about listening to waves crash, glasses clink, & the bored shouts of a bingo caller in the distance...

The end of the weekend but don't fret; embrace other cultures & you'll discover an excuse for a day off..... somewhere...

Thinking of moving to Spain? 10 THINGS YOU CAN LEAVE AT HOME & I´ve not even mentioned the mother-in-law...!

Sunday morning in Spain: It's so laid back here I've just had to shake the trees to wake the birds up...

Beware in Spain: When Brits flash headlights it means: "pull out my friend" When the Spanish do it´s: "COMING THROUGH! OUTTADAWAY!

An early morning coffee is a great idea in Spain...so long as the cafe bar owner has the same idea...

How ironic is it that some expats, who've lived here ages, make no attempt to speak Spanish but then say 'hola!' to me...

I know how upset the Spanish are over Gibraltar so to redress the balance we could give them say......... Eastbourne..?

Water off so tonight I'll wash on the rocks at Carabasi beach looking like a cross between a Timote ad...& a bison drinking...

Enjoy Spain. Think Spanish: we think: every day needs a timetable, they think: what's a timetable..?

To really enjoy Spain think like the Spanish, we think: 15mins late is rude. They think: 15mins late is early...

In the UK we worked around the clock, in Spain we work around meals...

Two people just came to the door in suits asking if I'd like to get closer to god, either they were hit men...or Jehovah's...

Went to Hercules CF this morning and no sign of corruption - although the president did win the toaster in the raffle...

If you don't hear from me for a while it's because I'm snowed under with work...& I hate getting sand in the phone... ;-)

Sussed it! If I have a siesta today I can justify another coffee

A bit sunburned today so I'm using natural Spanish remedies; Aloe Vera for the outside...& Rioja for the inside...

Anyone still not sure about moving to Spain? Last night I had to turn TV up cos the waves were so loud!

I know today isn't officially a holiday but yesterday was & I thought about work (a bit)...so I'm taking today in lieu...

Spain may be in recession but so is most of the planet...& I know where I'd rather be working my way through it

A look of respect from the TWO doormen at hotel when I asked for a room for ALL night, it was then I realised it was a brothel...

Off for a meeting at the town hall with the mayor & co... 'Smart casual' includes flip flops as far as I'm concerned...

As you know by now I don't often complain about Spain so if someone could move this cloud along? Ta

I'm going to have to get a new wine glass -apparently, my neighbour tells me, it's bad etiquette to drink Rioja from a snoopy mug...

Expats work for a lot less than they would get in the UK & work a lot harder...but not on weekends, or when the beach is open :-)

Woooohoooo! Spain's just switched the sun on...again!

You gotta love the Spanish winter...when you get a bit cold just head outside and make like a lizard...

So hot so cool, so relax, so late! So you so eat, so much, so soon? So ready so party, so sorry, so dizzy, So Europe, so us, so come,

There's a good few items drivers should have in their vehicle in Spain, don't buy a Mini...

Just went to town hall to see if (by chance) councillors were still around, cleaners looked at me as if I'd been eating stupid pie...

An unfortunate dodgy thermostat has seen my towns aquarium get too hot...the good news is you can now get piranha & chips for 5€...

Friday in Spain means swapping the morning mouse mat and coffee for an afternoon beach towel & Tinto...

Perhaps Marbella town hall could lead by example and but put bars over all its windows, lock them in & make them do what they're paid for

Just love it that directions in Spain are often: '...left at the first brothel & you'll find us just behind the next one on the left.'

It's mornings like this that I often remember the hustle & bustle of working in the UK...& then I have another coffee and forget

Friday....and according to my Spanish watch the weekend started about 4 hours ago... feels good to be late... ;-)

Sun shining, coffee drinking, Market shopping, menu eating, Wine sipping, siesta napping, Friend making, happy ending, is refreshing

You know you're in Spain when...they frown at you wanting a take away coffee...

An Alicante 'authentic' Irish bar I patronized last night ran out of Guinness so he offered that other 'Irish' speciality...cider

Winter in Gran Alacant means walking clean beaches next to the Med...Getting refreshed inside and out...

Wednesday...or the half time break, as we like to say in Spain

Still light, still warm, still wine... so Spain

The rain in Spain falls mainly on the brain... Do what successful expats do: open your mind & let the sunshine in..!

It's Thursday! So nearly Friday & therefore (expat rules apply here) counts as the weekend! Beach it is then!

For anyone not sure about moving to Spain...bear in mind: I got a tan this morning while eating my Sugar Puffs :-)

Mojitos are most definitely Spain´s answer to Marmite...

The main reason expats struggle with the lingo in Spain is because they don't learn it..! It seems they somehow expect to absorb it...

Don't be fooled when you come to Spain...those are not Wind Farms you see on the hills. They're just big fans to keep us cool :-)

Why do we live in Spain? They celebrate anything & everything here...full moon, new moon, cloudy day, the dog's dead... :-)

If there´s one piece of advice I would offer anyone thinking of moving to Spain it would have to be: ´Go with the Flow!

The Spanish are very persuasive: every time I go to a café in the countryside I end up buying a knife big enough to bring down a bison...

Spain is a country that constantly throws surprises at you...and the vast majority of them are good

Woohoo! A free weekend....tomorrow I intend to land on the beach and spread myself over a large area...

Shorts on, lunch, wine & music outside with friends & kids playing...and the thought of no long trousers till November. Welcome to Spain :-)

Tonight (once again) I will unselfishly dedicate the evening to helping the struggling Spanish economy...through the medium of Rioja...

We've reached that time of year in Spain when we all get religious & head for the beach, lay down a towel & worship our Sun God...

I think you'll find that somewhere in Spain today there will be a fiesta - & therefore I'm supporting it... :-)

Aha Friday! The day when everyone starts winding down for the weekend...but this is Spain so we started taking it easy Tuesday lunchtime...

Just got in to town and I've realised that parking in Spain is clearly not about getting it straight...but having your own style...

One of those little reminders of why you live in Spain: going to work in flip-flops... :-)

I live in a country that relies heavily on its wine industry so I'm darned if I'm not gonna show some respect & try most of it...

Reason #4764 for living in Spain: the only time you'll need to wear a suit is to YOUR funeral...or if you're being sentenced...

That's the summer wardrobe bought...luckily they had change for a tenner...

Dealing with Movistar 'customer service' is a bit like asking an aunt (who doesn't like you) for some money...

Be cool in Spain...don't be a tourist abroad - be a fan of a country that (if you let it) welcomes you with a slap on the back & a smile...

Living in Spain we have a 'snatch bag' that can be grabbed quickly like the emergency services. Although ours contains a towel & Ambre Soler

Funny expats: instead of going to all the trouble of learning one word a bloke today shouted 'post office' then mimed posting a letter...

Going to a meeting in a bit, in a bar on the beach...of course I shall be wearing a tie - but only to hold my shorts up...

Spain... there´s been a lot of talk of ´Cowboys´ & dodgy tradesmen...so just how do they get their ´Gatwick Diploma´..?

Reasons for living in Spain #67902 they think of everything! - they even bury you quick to make more room for the rest of us... :-)

All the while Spain acts like a wife - who's rich husband is now poor but still goes & gets her hair and nails done - it'll struggle...

Just had a great British brekky in Times Square...or as the Spanish call it: 'the whole farmland, dead, on a plate...'

Make the effort to take it easy in Spain

Spain in the summer: Cracking! Charming, Cool, Comfy, Coffees, Chiringuitos, Cut-downs, Cuties, Crinklies...all with a capital Sea...

Spain's bank bailout: was it wise to put all that cash in banks in Spain - a country full of retired British bank robbers..?

It's been that hot here today that the dogs look like I poured them onto the patio...

When I called the Spanish TV guy at 1.15pm he said 'es la hora de comer' (lunch) - I wouldn't mind but so is 2.15, 3.15 & 4.15...

Another Saturday and yet another barbecue with loads of food running around and kids being eaten...or something like that...

Today's discussion: 'there's no point in working today...yesterday was the strike and tomorrow it's the weekend...so no point...'

If you want the starter to arrive with everyone else's & your main course before everyone else is on the coffee...avoid Spain

Thinking of moving to Spain & have some get-up-&-go? Come on over. Spain STILL is the land where opportunity knocks...if you listen...

Every day we all meet for breakfast and every day the breakfast lasts longer while the working day gets shorter...

Spain; yesterday we had our winter & today normal service is resumed...sunshine!

Spain as an expat is a great leveller - a community that welcomes all, whether I have a polo player on my shirt, or a wine stain... It just is

I've just parked outside the bank in space meant for motorbikes...kindly helped by Vicente the Local Policeman who said 'no rush'

Jeez....Spain is the only country I know of where you put your coat on to go indoors...

Spain is the type of country that will hug you...just as hard as you hug it...

Spain is a bit like a dog on a lead: pull it along and it resists, let it trot along at its own pace & everyone's happy...

'A foreign car, illegally parked, is not a good idea.' In fact, slapping an officer on the backside, with a banjo will draw less attention...

So far today: been running on beach, walked dogs, had breakfast on the terrace & now coffee with friends in the sun...how's UK guys...? ;-)

How is it that Movistar have a perfectly clear voice to answer 1004 & when you get a human its mayhem in a South American call centre...?

6 KIDS

So...that's the fence fixed, the draught excluded and the kids sitting quietly on the sofa...don't you just love Gaffa tape..?

My son has come home & complained about me eating all 10 jam donuts in the packet. Not considering for a minute the lesson I was teaching...

I have a teen... Free to a good home, house trained (ish), only one in litter - all jabs, doesn't wander off & can open fridge...

Note to son: If you think that you doing the washing up will leave me feeling I have no role in life..? It's a risk I'm willing to take...

Pointing and laughing was not the response I expected from my son when I asked about my new haircut......

I see my son has beaten me to the fridge (again)...I guess I should be grateful he doesn´t eat plastic...

My son (vehemently) denied procrastinating...until I explained that it wasn't something rude...

Bloody teenagers are like puppies...clumsy, sleepy, messy & incapable of fending for themselves - but at least the pup is cute...

Teenagers: the argument that no one else will see your room so you can leave the bed unmade every day...is actually a good one!

Getting your own back on kids: I walk in my son's room to meet his new mates dressed like the Fonz and go "heyyyy!"

Teenagers? "I forgot" "it´s soaking" "I was gonna do that" & "I didn´t see it" are crap excuses that didn´t work for me either...

Very windy today and the advice is to tie anything down that could move...the kids aren't happy, I'll untie them later... ;) #peace

In an age when monkeys can be taught to communicate and even perform tasks...I can't even get my teenage son to put the hose away properly...

Note for teenage son in morning: my day started 6 hours ago, put lid on toothpaste, realise we don't have a dishwasher, sleep well...

Either the cops have raided desperately searching for something & turned the place upside down - or my son popped home for a few minutes...

I tried explaining to my son; when I do the washing I throw away bits of loose thread...how was I to know it was his girlfriend's G-string..?

It's getting embarrassing. Once again I've locked myself out & had to ask my son to come home & let me in...Laughing was not the answer...

There is a buzz of anticipation in the air (or it may be the air con playing up)...

AVAILABLE NOW
www.amazon.com

It just is..

DAVE BULL

Spain 2010: dumped by his girlfriend, arrested by the Guardia, and a blind date with an aunt... just 364 days to go...

EXPAT LIFE REVEALED

Praise for *It just is...*

*At last! Someone has written a book about what life is really like living as an expat in Spain. Dave Bull's first book **It Just Is...** is an hilarious reminder of some of things that go on out here and in the book he recounts some of those typical experiences in Spain that we've all been through and takes a look at some of the interesting characters we get to meet in the expat community and beyond.* **Cliff Roberts, Real Radio FM**

You may even recognise someone (or yourself!) as Dave reveals the ups and downs of life...especially his!- **Coastrider newspaper**

*Many expat books concentrate on what a great life they're having in Spain but In **It just is...** Dave Bull humorously reveals what life is really like living as a foreigner on the Costa Blanca and the good, the bad and the downright ugly... and that brings me on to his disastrous attemots at meeting women in Spain which, I must admit, I laughed out loud at. Sorry Dave.* **Ali Meehan**

If you have any connection to Spain at all or want to show the folks back home just how interesting (and fun) life can be living as en expat then get this book. You'll find, like I did, that just after a few pages yourself nodding and saying, yes that happened to me too! **Steve Hall**

ABOUT THE BOOK

It's Spain. A country where it's considered dangerous to change lanes on a roundabout , but ok to buy a chainsaw in ALDI... in *It Just Is* Dave Bull takes a hilarious look at life as an expat in Spain.

Why do Brits behave differently when they move to Spain? And what are the funny (and sometimes annoying) differences in culture between us and 'them'?

Dave found out the hard (and funny) way...

At the end of 1999 Dave Bull reluctantly moved to Alicante with his wife and his 7 year old son to start a new life.

Ten years later his life has changed following his divorce and ***It Just Is...*** is a humorous account of a Dave's life living and working in Spain as a single dad, and looking for romance, and failing miserably.

While offering advice and help to expats Dave Bull recounts his experiences which included buying a house in the middle of nowhere (powered by car batteries) and working as the editor of a local newspaper (and making appointments with dead politicians).

And... coping with a teenager (and all his mates) in the house along with a Great Dane puppy that has its own set of rules (meet Mrs Jones) means that Dave's life is never simple as it perhaps could be.

In amongst it all he looks at how recent history has shaped modern Spain and, just as importantly, finds out just what the Spanish really think of expats!

It Just Is... is a must-read if you have any connection to Spain at all. Dave reveals the frustrations of dealing with Spanish banks, Spanish politics and Spanish lawyers. Then there's car hire, cyclists and religion. However, generously sprinkled in amongst the fun he provides some sound advice to expats and those thinking of making the move to Spain as well as his dealings (good and not so good) with the Guardia Civil... and then there's his love life...

It just is...

Available in paperback and on kindle from

www.amazon.com

A load of BULL

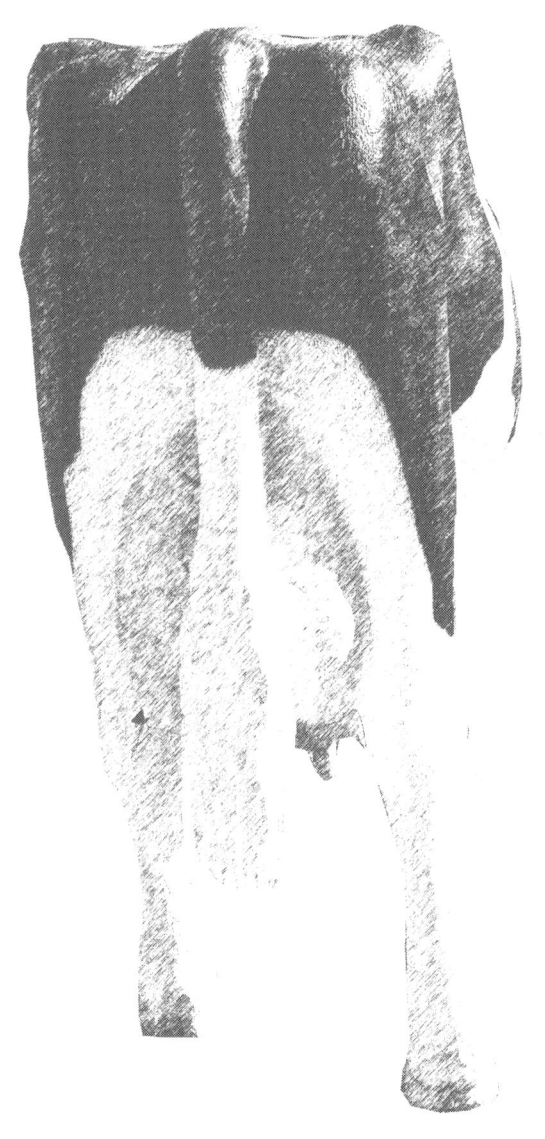

THE END

Printed in Great Britain
by Amazon.co.uk, Ltd.,
Marston Gate.